Ch 3-96

tennis

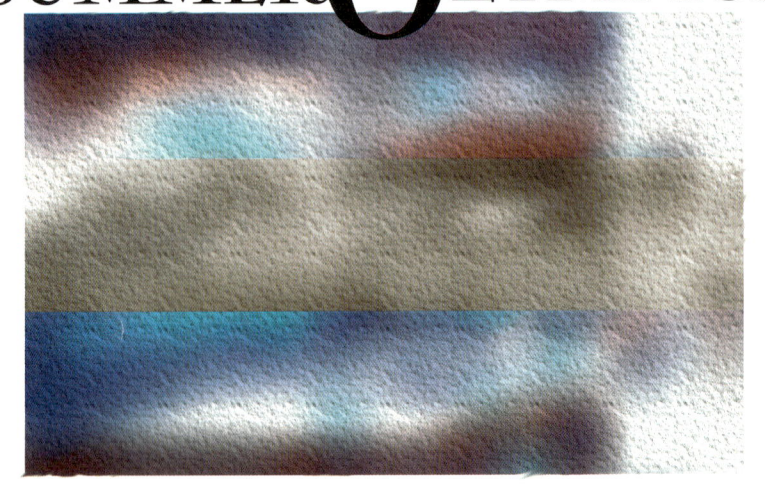

the
SUMMER OLYMPICS

tennis

SUMMER OLYMPICS

PUBLISHED BY SMART APPLE MEDIA

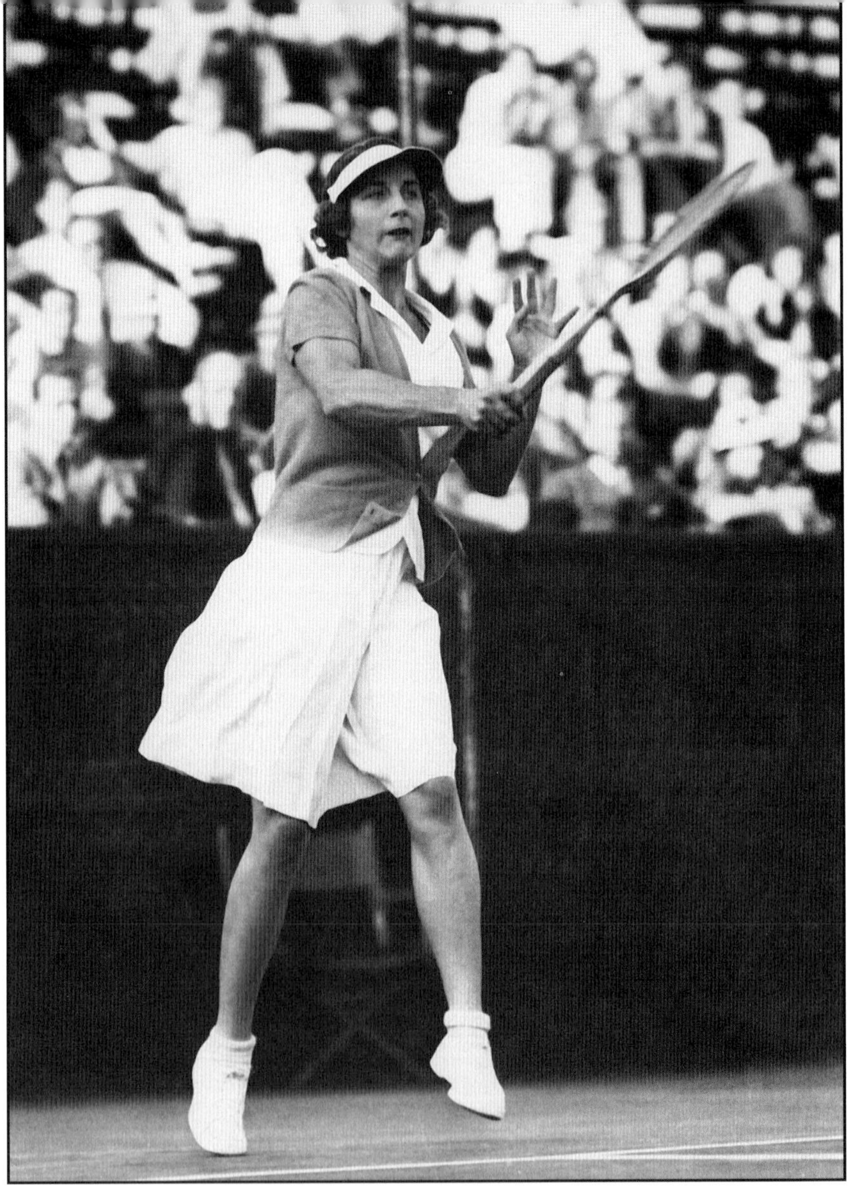

Published by Smart Apple Media
123 South Broad Street, Mankato, Minnesota 56001

Cover Illustration by Eric Melhorn

Designed by Core Design

Photos by: Bettmann Archives, Sports Photo Masters and Wide World Photos

Copyright © 1995 Smart Apple Media.
International copyrights reserved in all countries.
No part of this book may be reproduced in any form without written permission from the publisher.
Printed in the United States of America.

Library of Congress Cataloging-in-Publication Data

DiMeglio, Steve.
Tennis / by Steve DiMeglio.
(The Summer Olympics)
Includes index.
Summary: Traces the history of tennis as an Olympic sport.

ISBN 1-887068-07-4

1. Tennis—Juvenile literature. 2. Olympics—Juvenile literature. [1. Tennis—History. 2. Olympics.] I. Title. II. Series.

GV996.5.D55 1995   95-11967
796.342—dc20

Stefan Edberg won the men's singles in 1984.

CAUSING A RACKET

Tennis is one of the world's most popular sports. Fans love to watch the best players in the world hit the tennis ball at top speeds and run down impossible shots—dreaming that they, too, could play like the greats.

Tennis demands strength, speed, agility and endurance. Top-level players can hit the ball up to 130 miles per hour (209

Having tennis back in the Olympics is a victory for players and fans alike.

km/hr). They can make the tennis ball spin away from a player and even into a player. Some players rush to the net after a good serve, putting pressure on their opponents as they slam the ball back in an instant. Others rely more on playing the back of the court, wearing their opponents down by hitting the ball back consistently until the opponent makes a mistake.

The drama of tennis attracts thousands of fans to tournaments throughout the world, and millions more watch on television. Now, after a long absence, tennis is being celebrated in the Olympics as well, and fans of the sport are convinced that tennis is in the Olympics to stay. The Olympic Games offer great players the chance to represent their countries in time-honored competition—and offer tennis fans another venue to watch the world's best.

In 1996, that venue will be in the United States in Atlanta. The 1996 Summer Olympic Games are likely to attract well-known tennis stars such as Germany's Steffi Graf and Boris Becker, Sweden's Stefan Edberg, Spain's Arantxa Sanchez Vicario and the United States' Andre Agassi and Pete Sampras.

Their goal? An Olympic gold medal, and all the honor and prestige it represents.

Chris Evert supports Olympic tennis competition (pages 10-11).

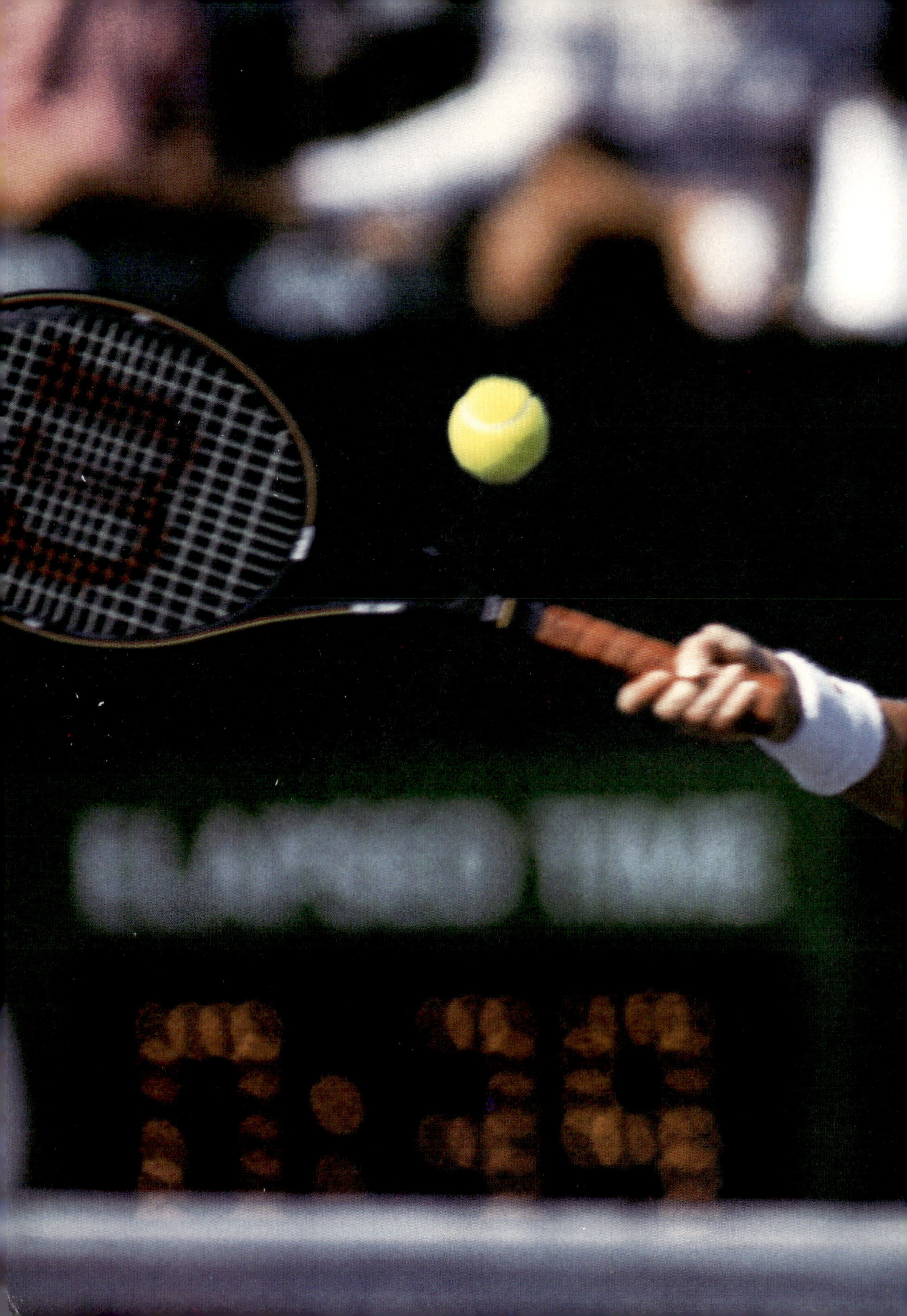

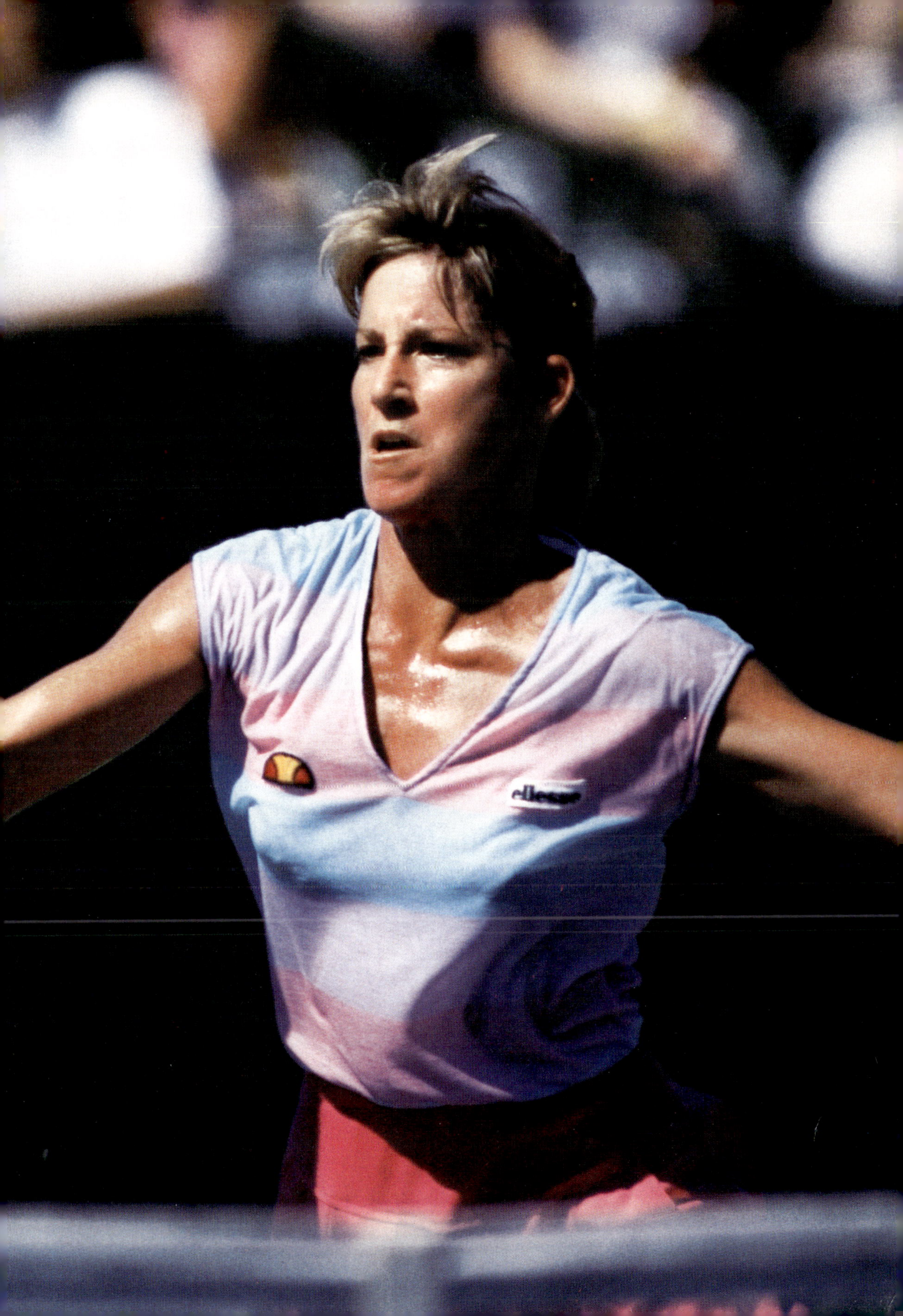
ellesse

THE EARLY YEARS

Tennis as it is played today developed in England in the late 1800s. Men's tennis was one of the original sports in the first modern Olympic Games, held in Athens, Greece, in 1896. Women's tennis was added four years later.

In the beginning, the world's best players did not consider the Olympics an important tournament, so many did not

Superstar Bill Tilden never played in the Olympics.

Suzanne Lenglen gracefully dominated tennis in the 1920s.

play. In fact, not one top player in the world even went to the 1912 Olympics in Stockholm because the Olympics were at the same time as the Wimbledon Championships, the most highly regarded tournament in the world.

There were some highlights in the early years, however. Ireland's John Pius Boland entered the 1896 Olympics at the last minute and won gold medals in both singles and doubles. In 1900 in Paris, the first Olympics in which women competed, Charlotte "Chattie" Cooper of Great Britain—who would eventually win five Wimbledon titles—became the first female Olympic champion.

At the 1920 Olympics in Antwerp, Suzanne Lenglen of France showed why she was one of the greatest women's players of all time. The eventual winner of six Wimbledon singles titles and six French Open singles championships hardly broke a sweat. In the 10 sets it took her to win the gold medal, she lost only four games. "This is a beautiful gold medal. I'm glad I came and played in this tournament," Lenglen said after winning.

And Helen Wills Moody—the best women's player from 1923 to 1938—added two gold medals to her trophy collection at the 1924 Games in Paris by winning in both women's singles and doubles.

World-class tennis action returned to the Olympics in 1984.

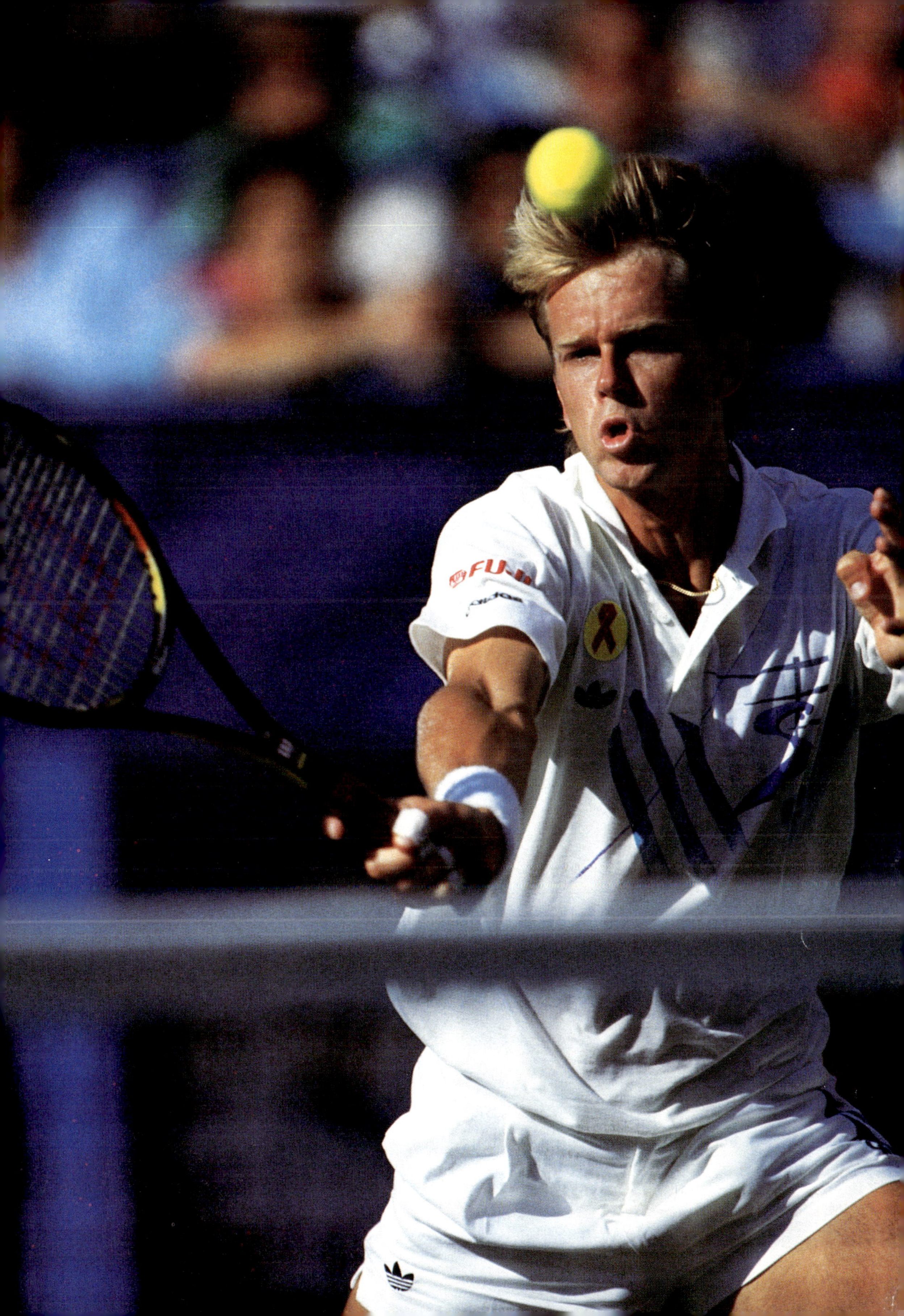

But these great moments could not save tennis. After the 1924 Olympics, conflicts between the different governing bodies of tennis led to the sport's elimination from the Games. Because of these off-court battles, some great players—such as Bill Tilden, Bjorn Borg, and Billie Jean King—never got the chance to play in the Olympics.

TENNIS RETURNS

In 1968 in Mexico City, tennis was played at the Olympics for the first time in 44 years. The sport did not count in the medals race—it was played only as a demonstration sport because Olympic officials wanted to see if tennis was popular enough to bring it back. There wasn't much interest. Crowds were small and the game's best players did not compete.

Over the years, however, tennis has grown in popularity around the world, thanks to the Grand Slam tournaments—the Wimbledon Championships in England, the Australian Open in Australia, the French Open in France, and the U.S. Open in the United States. Worldwide tournaments pitting country against country, such as the Davis Cup and the Federation Cup, have also attracted attention to the sport, as has ever-increasing television coverage.

Finally, the International Olympic Committee agreed to let tennis come back to the Olympics as a demonstration sport in 1984. Only players 20 years or younger could play. But for the first

Tennis requires strength, stamina and control.

time in any sport in Olympic history, professionals were allowed to compete. It was a controversial decision. Some thought pros would ruin the Olympics. Others said the Olympics should be for the best players in the world, regardless of their status. "It's about time we let in the pros," one official said.

Despite the controversy, the fans were happy. Every ticket in the 8,500-seat arena in Los Angeles was sold each of the six

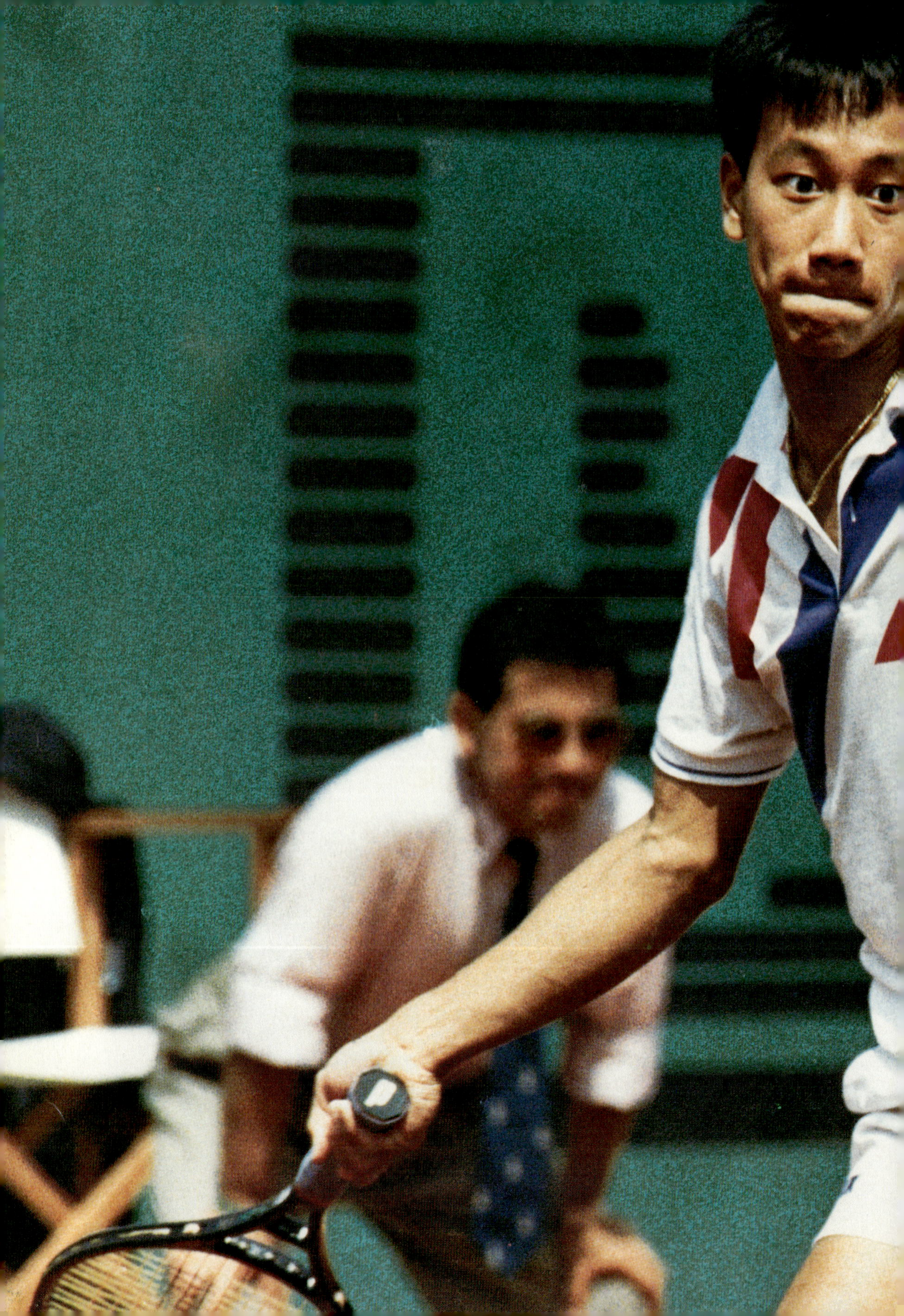

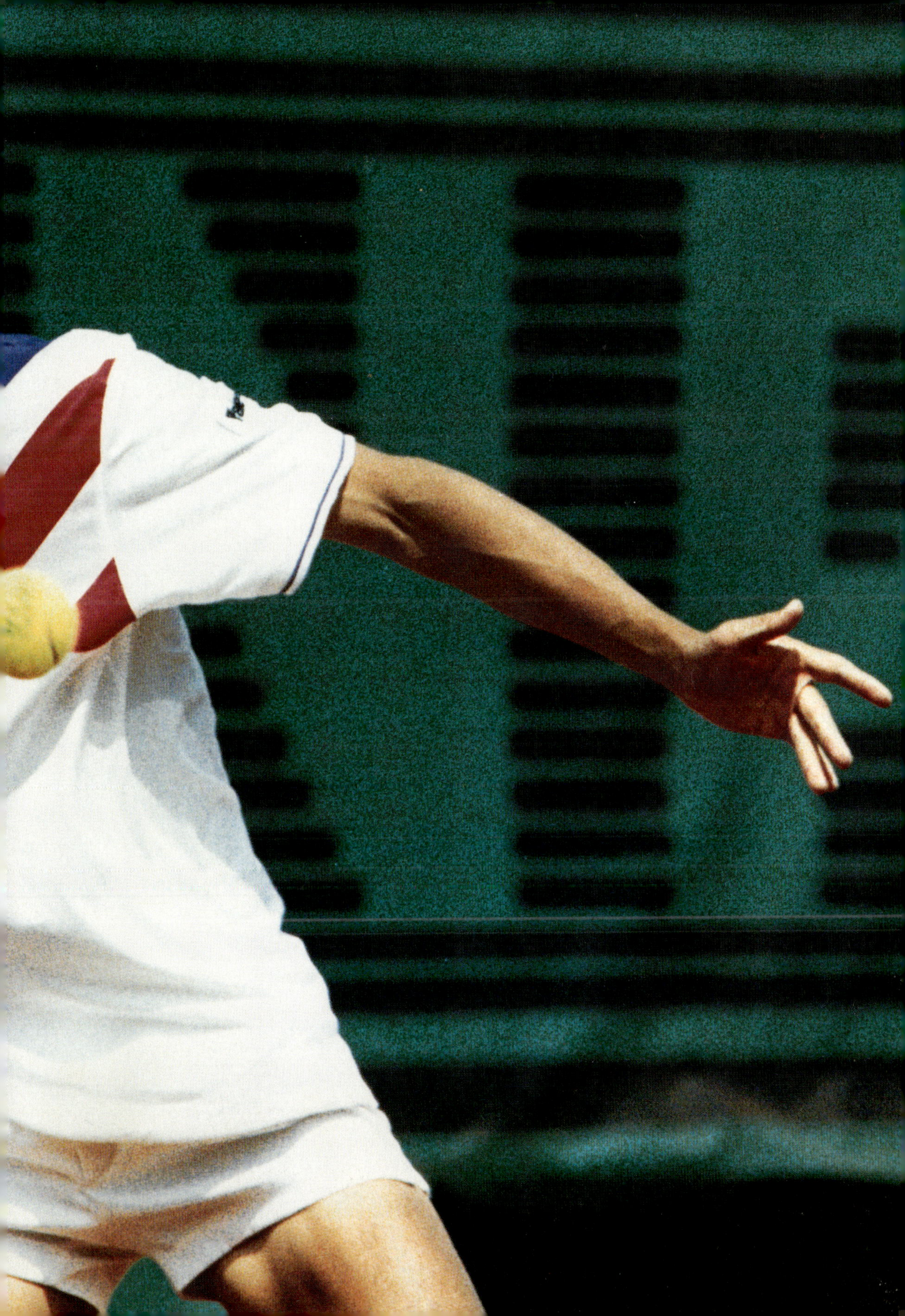

days of competition. Only singles tennis was played. Stefan Edberg of Sweden won the men's title with great play at the net and Steffi Graf of West Germany easily won the women's title.

GOLDEN SLAM

Steffi Graf was only 15 years old when she won the Olympic demonstration tournament in 1984. Just three years later, she was ranked No. 1 in the world, relying on punishing ground strokes and a big serve. Then, in the 1988 Seoul Olympics, Graf capped a year like no other player—male or female—has ever experienced.

That year, for the first time since 1924, tennis had official status in the Olympics. Graf came to Seoul after having won the Australian Open, the French Open, Wimbledon and the U.S. Open, becoming only the fifth player in history to win the Grand Slam. Then she won the gold at the Olympics as well, winning the first-ever "Golden Slam."

"This is special," Graf said after getting her gold medal, acknowledging the significance of Olympic competition. "I've won a lot of big tournaments and this is one of them."

In the men's singles tournament, Czechoslovakia's Miloslav Mecir gave a clinic in playing tennis from the baseline. His precise ground strokes wore down his opponents. He upset heavy favorite Stefan Edberg of Sweden in the semifinals and then beat American Tim Mayotte in the finals for the gold medal.

In doubles, Americans swept the competition. Pam Shriver and Zina Garrison won a three-set thriller over Czechoslovakia's Jana Novotna and Helena Sukova. Ken Flach and Robert Seguso beat Spain's Emilio Sanchez and Sergio Casal in a five-set marathon that lasted nearly four hours.

Steffi Graf took the women's singles titles in 1984 and 1988.

DREAM TEEN

Tennis still faced some growing pains when the Olympics arrived in Barcelona in 1992. While there were no rules about the age of players, a new rule said players must have played in a Davis Cup or a Federation Cup in 1990 or 1991 to be able to play in the Olympics. This rule prevented great players like Martina Navratilova, Monica Seles, Gabriela Sabatini and others from competing.

Stealing the spotlight that year was Jennifer Capriati of the United States, who at 16 was already one of the top players in the world. She showed why in Barcelona, using her quickness and powerful strokes to overcome the field and 110-degree (43 °C) temperatures on the red clay surface. Capriati beat hometown favor-

Sampras (above) and Becker (right) are stars of the '90s.

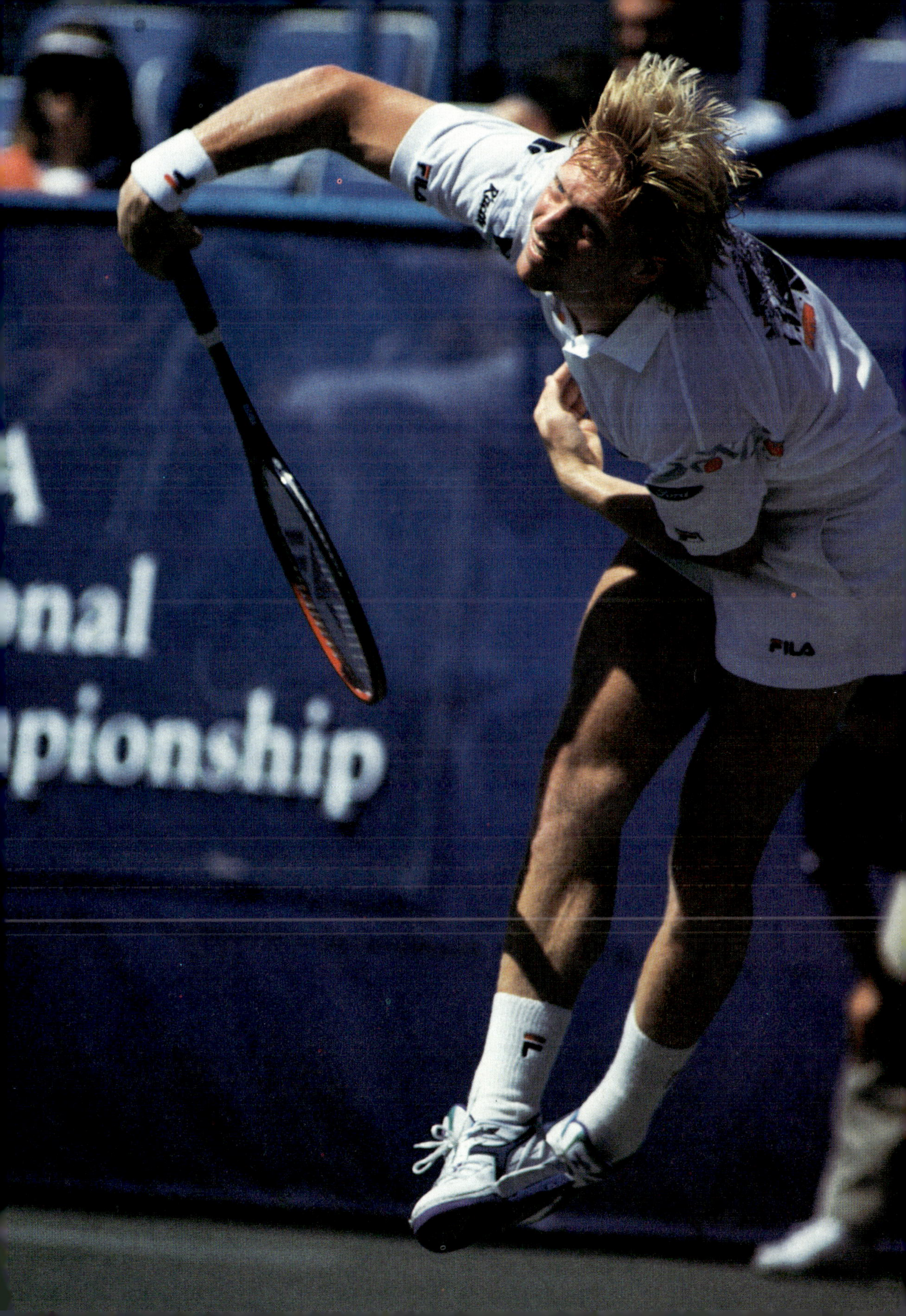
onal
pionship
FILA

Jim Courier will be back in 1996.

ite Arantxa Sanchez Vicario in the semifinals. In the finals, she lost her first set against Graf but came back to win the final two sets to become the youngest player ever to win an Olympic tennis title.

"I can hardly believe it," Capriati said after winning. "It was cool. This is the greatest win of my life."

Capriati wasn't the only winner. Tennis was a winner, too. Crowds of 15,000 jammed the tennis center to watch during every day of the tennis competition.

In the men's tournament, shocking upsets stunned the world. American Jim Courier was the No. 1 ranked player in the world. He lost. So did U.S. stars Pete Sampras and Michael Chang. Sweden's Stefan Edberg lost in the first round. Germany's Boris Becker and Michael Stich were victims as well. In fact, not one of the top 20 players in the world made it to the finals, in which Switzerland's Marc Rosset beat Spain's Jordi Arrese.

Becker and Stich teamed to win the men's doubles, though, and Americans Mary Joe Fernandez and Gigi Fernandez (no relation) won the women's doubles.

BIGGER THINGS TO COME

As the Olympic Games head toward the 21st century, tennis has a firm grip on Olympic tradition. "When you play for your country, it's the best feeling in the world," American player

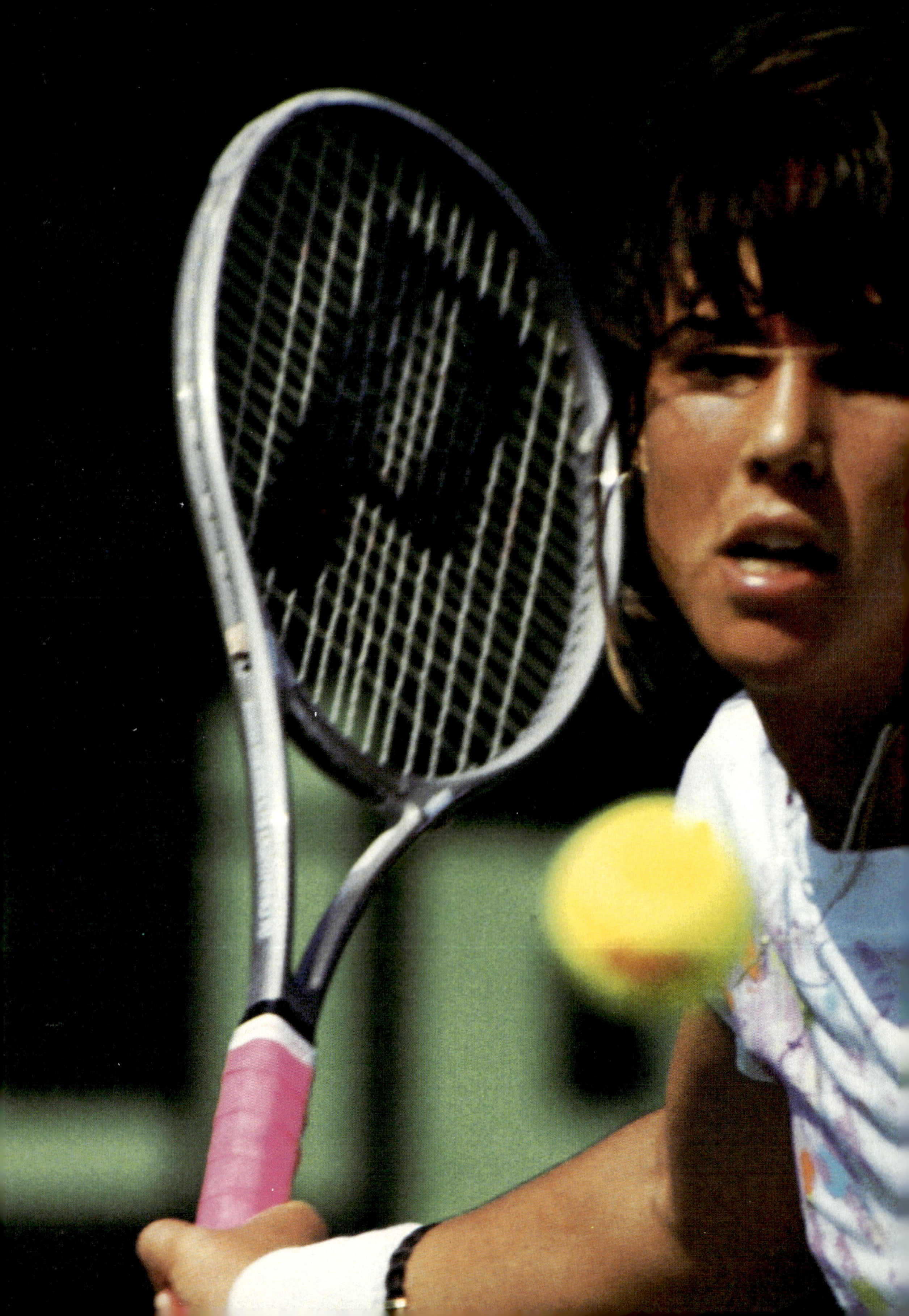

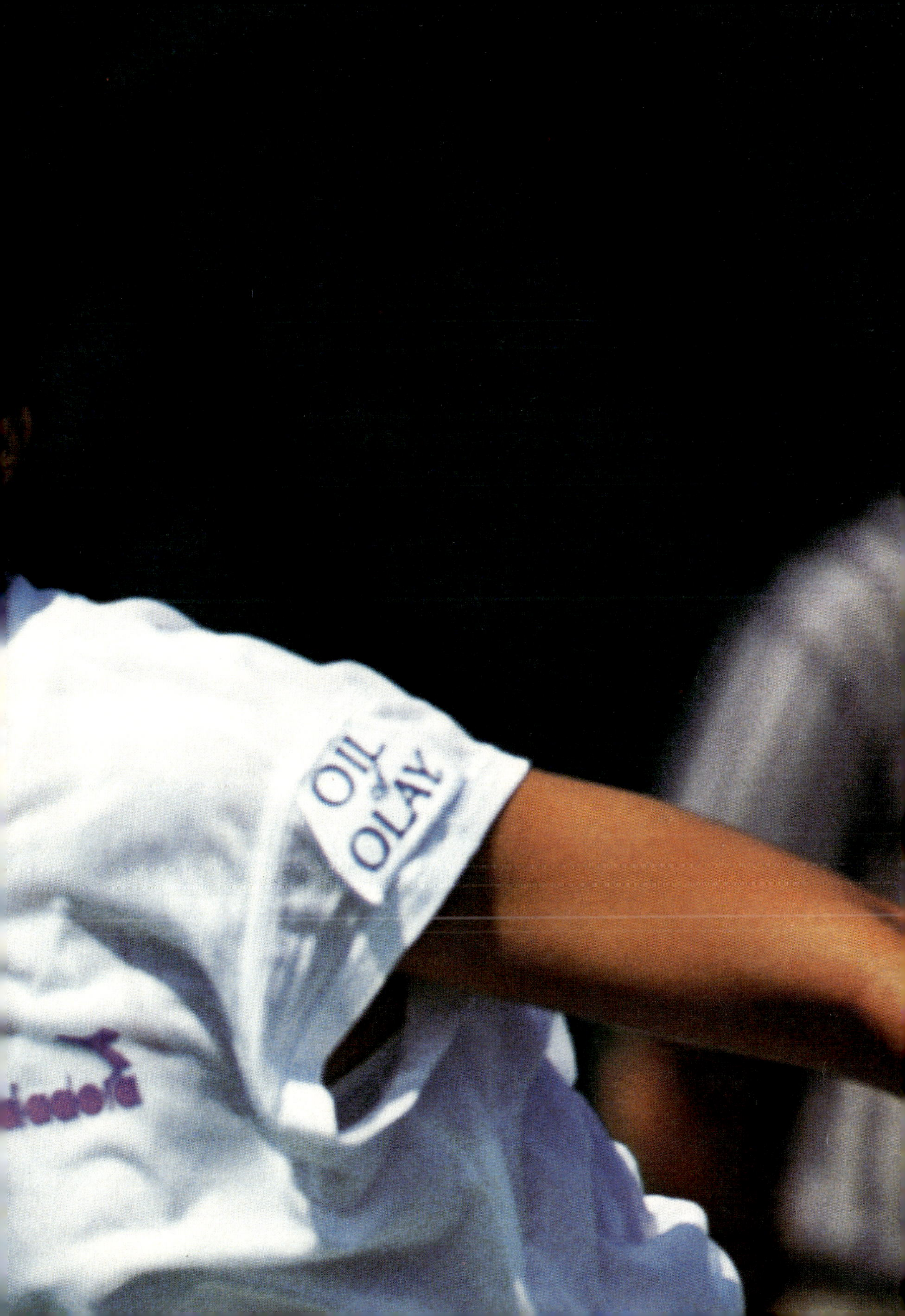
OIL OLAY

John McEnroe said. "When players realize that, they will be begging to play in the Olympics."

Chris Evert, an American professional who competed in the 1988 Olympics, agreed. "I think it could be as big or even bigger than the Grand Slam tournaments," the all-time great said. "Alongside all the other sports, it could become spectacular."

In the future, there may be more changes for the sport. Germany's Boris Becker thinks the tournament would be better if countries played as teams. That suggestion is being discussed for the 1996 Olympics in Atlanta.

If tennis goes to a team format, the United States could feature superstars Pete Sampras, Andre Agassi, Jim Courier and Gigi Fernandez. Germany could be a superpower with Boris Becker, Michael Stich, Steffi Graf and Anke Huber. Spain could come with a lineup of stars like Sergi Bruguera, Arantxa Sanchez Vicario and Conchita Martinez. Russia could rule with top players Natalia Zvereva, Andrei Medvedev and Yevgeny Kafelnikov.

Whatever changes take place in the structure of the competition, Olympic tennis seems to have a bright future. "I have no doubts that tennis is here to stay in the Olympics," said Philippe Chatrier, president of the International Tennis Federation.

After the 1992 Olympics, interest in the sport is at an all-time high. Who knows what victories await in 1996?

SUMMER GAMES CHAMPIONS:

tennis

Men's Competition - Singles

Year	Player	Country
1896	John Pius Boland	Britain/Ireland
1900	Hugh Doherty	Britain
1904	Beals Wright	USA
1908	Josiah Ritchie	Britain
	Arthur Gore (indoor courts)	Britain
1912	Charles Winslow	S. Africa
	Andre Gobert (indoor courts)	France
1920	Louis Raymond	S. Africa
1924	Vincent Richards	USA
1988	Miloslav Mecir	Czechoslovakia
1992	Marc Rosset	Switzerland

Doubles

Year	Player	Country
1896	J.P. Boland, F. Traun	Ireland/Germany
1900	R. Doherty, H. Doherty	Britain
1904	E. Leonard, B. Wright	USA
1908	G. Hillyard, R. Doherty	Britain
	A. Gore, H. Roper-Barrett (indoor courts)	Britain
1912	C. Winslow, H. Kitson	S. Africa
	A. Gobert, M. Germot (indoor courts)	France
1920	O. N. Turnbull, M. Woosnam	Britain
1924	V. Richards, F. Hunter	USA
1988	K. Flach, R. Seguso	USA
1992	B. Becker, M. Stich	Germany

tennis

RECORDS

Women's Competition - Singles

Year	Player	Country
1900	Charlotte Cooper	Britain
1904	(event not held)	
1908	Dorothy Chambers	Britain
	Gwendolyn Eastlake-Smith (indoor courts)	Britain
1912	Marguerite Broquedis	France
	Edith Hannam (indoor courts)	Britain
1920	Suzanne Lenglen	France
1924	Helen Wills	USA
1988	Steffi Graf	W. Germany
1992	Jennifer Capriati	USA

Doubles

Year	Player	Country
1920	W. M. McNair, K. McKane	Britain
1924	H. Wightman, H. Wills	USA
1988	P. Shriver, Z. Garrison	USA
1992	M.J. Fernandez, G. Fernandez	USA

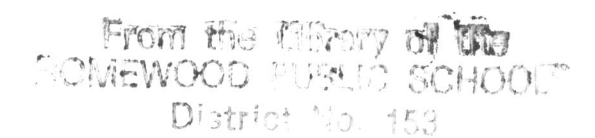

INDEX

Agassi, Andre, 9, 28
Antwerp Games (1920), 13-14
Arrese, Jordi, 25
Athens Games (1896), 12, 13
Atlanta Games (1996), 9, 28
Australian Open, 16, 20

Barcelona Games (1992), 22
Becker, Boris, 9, 25, 28
Boland, John Pius, 13
Borg, Bjorn, 16
Bruguera, Sergi, 28

Capriati, Jennifer, 22, 25
Casal, Sergio, 21
Chang, Michael, 25
Chatrier, Philippe, 28
Cooper, Charlotte, 13
Courier, Jim, 25, 28

Davis Cup, 16, 22

Edberg, Stefan, 9, 20-21, 25
Evert, Chris, 28

Federation Cup, 16, 22
Fernandez, Gigi, 25, 28
Fernandez, Mary Joe, 25
Flach, Ken, 21
French Open, 14, 16, 20

Garrison, Zina, 21
Golden Slam, 20-21
Graf, Steffi, 9, 20, 25, 28
Grand Slam, 16, 20

Huber, Anke, 28

International Olympic Committee, 16

Kafelnikov, Yevgeny, 28
King, Billie Jean, 16

Lenglen, Suzanne, 13-14
Los Angeles Games (1984), 17, 19

Martinez, Conchita, 28
Mayotte, Tim, 21
McEnroe, John, 28
Mecir, Miloslav, 20-21
Medvedev, Andrei, 28

men's competition
  doubles champions, 21, 25
  singles champions, 13, 20-21, 25
Mexico City Games (1968), 16
Moody, Helen Wills, 14

Navratilova, Martina, 22
Novotna, Jana, 21

Paris Games (1900), 13
Paris Games (1924), 14

Rosset, Marc, 25

Sabatini, Gabriela, 22
Sampras, Pete, 9, 25, 28
Sanchez, Emilio, 21
Sanchez Vicario, Arantxa, 9, 25, 28
Seguso, Robert, 21
Seles, Monica, 22
Seoul Games (1988), 20
Shriver, Pam, 21
Stich, Michael, 25, 28
Stockholm Games (1912), 13
Sukova, Helena, 21
Sweden, 9, 20, 25

tennis
  future of, 25, 28
  Olympic history, 12-17
  popularity growth, 16, 25
  pro participation, 17
  skills, 7, 9
  team possibilities, 28
  youngest Olympic title winner, 25
Tilden, Bill, 16

United States
  doubles champions, 21
  tennis stars, 9, 25, 28
  women champions, 14, 22, 25
U.S. Open, 16, 20

Vicario, Arantxa Sanchez. See Sanchez Vicario, Arantxa

Wimbledon, 13, 16, 20
women's competition
  doubles champions, 21, 25
  first Olympic champion, 13, 14
  singles champions, 14, 20, 22, 25
  youngest Olympic title winner, 25

Zvereva, Natalia, 28